mormon
ORIGAMI

todd huisken

mormon
ORIGAMI

CFI
An Imprint of Cedar Fort, Inc.
SPRINGVILLE, UTAH

ISBN 13: 978-1-4621-1339-2

Published by CFI, an imprint of Cedar Fort, Inc.
2373 W. 700 S., Springville, UT 84663
Distributed by Cedar Fort, Inc., www.cedarfort.com

LIBRARY OF CONGRESS CATALOGING-IN-PUBLICATION DATA

Huisken, Todd, 1968- author.
Mormon origami / Todd Huisken.
pages cm
Cover title: ©2013
ISBN 978-1-4621-1339-2
1. Origami. 2. Church of Jesus Christ of Latter-day Saints--In art. 3. Mormon Church--In art. I. Title. II. Title: ©2013.

TT872.5.H85 2013
736'.982--dc23

2013023180

Cover and interior design by Shawnda T. Craig
Cover design © 2013 Lyle Mortimer
Edited by Emily S. Chambers

Printed in the United States of America

10 9 8 7 6 5 4 3 2 1

Printed on acid-free paper

This book is dedicated to the love of my life & my very best friend. Jill. & to the four greatest kids a dad could ever have: Kylie. Jolie. Sophie & Dean.

Special thanks to Andrew Hudson for his amazing designs & artwork. & Nick Robinson for his artwork. Additionally. special thanks to several individuals who inspired this book: Brett Shaw. Chandler Newby. Daniel Carter & William Phelps.

CONTENTS

INTRODUCTION
to origami

Origami (pronounced or-i-GA-me) is a Japanese word that means "to fold paper" & is known as the Japanese art of folding paper into shapes representing objects. Paper folding has been practiced for thousands of years & first began between AD 100 & 200 in China. But even though origami began in China, it didn't become widely popular until the Japanese took a liking to it in AD 600.

In the beginning, when paper was first invented & expensive, origami was used for religious ceremonies such as weddings & Chinese tea ceremonies, but today origami can be found in all types of settings, such as schools, churches, art galleries, museums, & if you watch carefully you can even spot origami figures on television.

You'll notice that each origami design in this book has a skill level listed at the top of the page. Skill level 1 is the easiest, so start there, & then work your way up to the skill level 3 designs, which are the most challenging. An index at the back of the book will help you find designs based on skill level.

I hope you enjoy folding the designs in this book, which come from stories in the Book of Mormon, LDS Church history & modern-day temples.

ORIGAMI

FOLDS

FOLDS

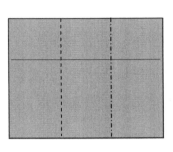
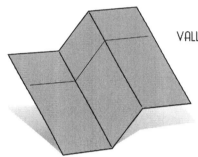

VALLEY FOLDS are represented by a dashed line:
MOUNTAIN FOLDS by a dot-dash line.
PRECREASES are shown with a thin line
that does not touch the sides.
All FOLDED or RAW EDGES are
shown with a thick line.

A RABBIT-EAR is a procedure where
four folds are made at once. meeting
at a vertex. Generally you will
precrease all four of them.
and flatten the fourth into place.

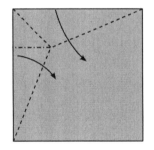
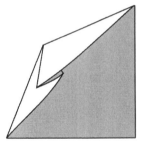

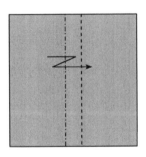

A PLEAT creates two creases.
one mountain & one valley.
Usually the mountain is
precreased & the valley is
flattened into place.

FOLDS

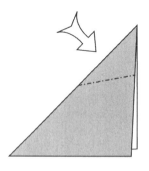 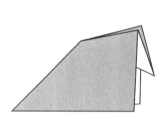

INSIDE REVERSE FOLDS change the direction of the spine
of a flap. adding two creases along the way.

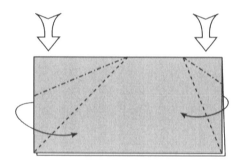 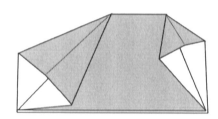

SQUASH FOLDS are made by taking the spine of a flap. opening it up
& flattening it. Usually the valley crease is precreased.

FOLDS

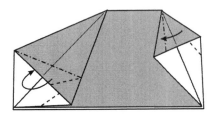 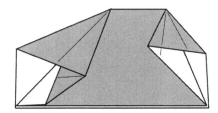

A SWIVEL fold takes an area of paper & pivots it around a vertex.
Swivel folds fall into the same group of operations as squash & reverse folds.

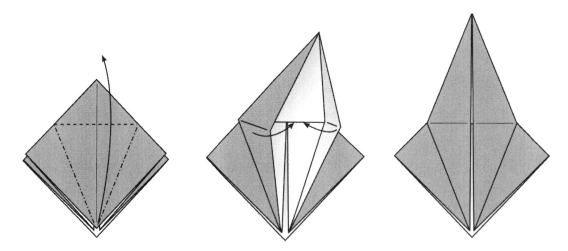

A PETAL fold is like doing two squash folds at once.
This is difficult, so try to precrease as much of it as possible first.

6

BOOK OF MORMON

— DESIGNS —

TREE
of Life

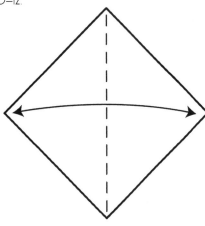

1. Start with a square piece of paper.
Fold & unfold.

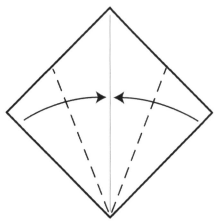

2. Fold sides to center line.

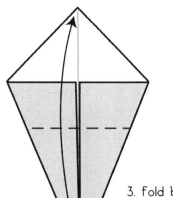

3. Fold bottom
point to top point.

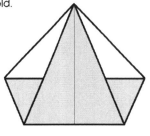

4. Turn over.

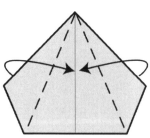

5. Fold sides to center line.

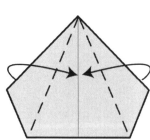

6. Fold top
layer down.

TREE
of Life

QUIZ YOURSELF:
Can you name the members of Lehi's family who ate the fruit from the tree of life?

Nephi 8:14-15

ANSWER:
Sariah, Sam, Nephi

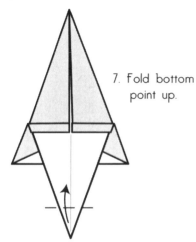

7. Fold bottom point up.

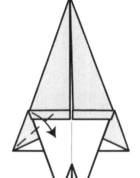

8. Fold corner of top layer down.

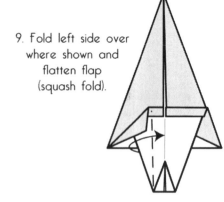

9. Fold left side over where shown and flatten flap (squash fold).

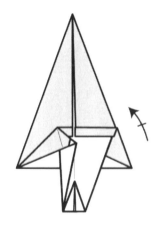

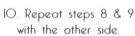

10. Repeat steps 8 & 9 with the other side.

11. Fold top point down & side points in.

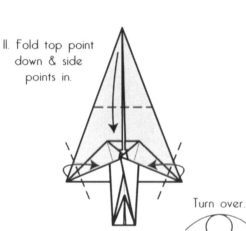

Turn over.

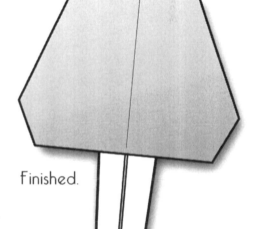

Finished.

artwork: Nick Robinson

9

DID YOU KNOW?

Most swords in early America were shorter in length & mostly made of a stone called "obsidian" & wood.

SWORD
of Laban

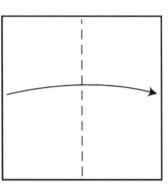

1. Start with a square piece of paper. Fold in half.

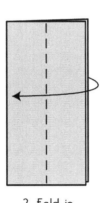

2. Fold in half again.

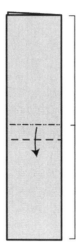

3. Using two folds, pleat top half over bottom half.

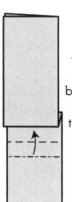

4. Using two folds, pleat the bottom half over the top so the folded edges meet.

5. Fold & unfold the four corners of the top layer.

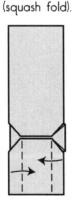

6. Fold sides over & squash flaps flat (squash fold).

7. Fold top corners down to make a point.

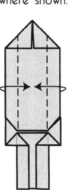

8. Fold sides toward middle where shown.

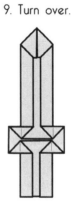

9. Turn over.

Finished.

artwork: Nick Robinso

LIAHONA

DID YOU KNOW?
The Liahona is also called the
"ball", "director" & "compass"
in the Book of Mormon.

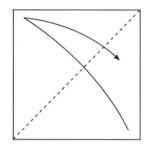

1. Start with a square piece
of paper. Fold & unfold.

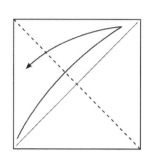

2. Fold in half the other
way & unfold.

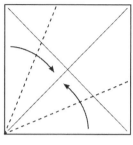

3. Fold sides to
center line.

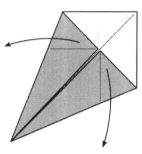

4. Unfold.

5. Repeat step 3 & 4
on the lower right corner.

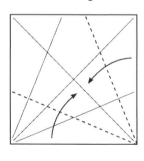

6. Repeat step 3 & 4
on the upper right corner.

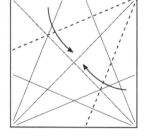

7. Repeat step 3 & 4
on the upper left corner

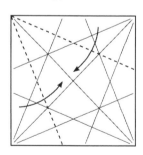

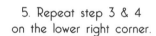

11

LIAHONA

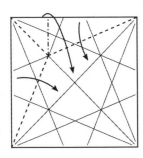

8. Using the creases already made, fold the left side & top toward the middle of the paper. This will create a flap in the middle. Pinch the crease of the flap & fold the flap over to the right side (rabbit ear).

9. Fold the flap back up to the center, then opening the flap slightly, press the paper flat (squash fold).

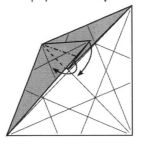

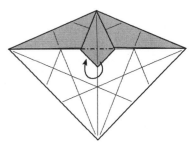

10. Tuck the triangle flap underneath.

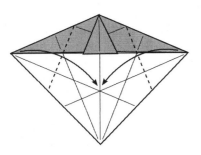

11. Fold sides in along the crease so their points meet in the center.

12. Fold bottom up & tuck inside.

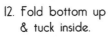

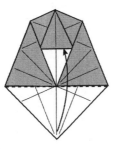

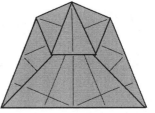

13. Turn over.

14. Fold the bottom corners up using creases.

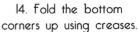

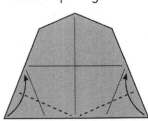

LIAHONA

skill level: 2

DID YOU KNOW?

The word *Liahona* means "compass."

Alma 37:38

15. Fold and unfold the corner at the dotted line, making a crease on both sides. Then at the arrow, push the corner inside (reverse fold).

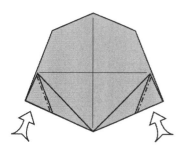

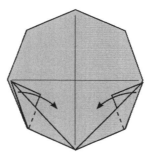

16. Fold points toward center.

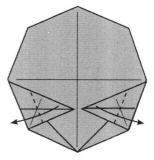

17. Fold points back out to sides.

18. Turn over.

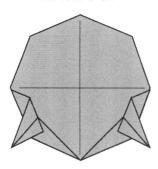

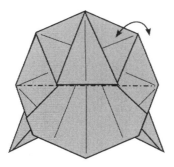

19. Fold back & forth to establish a strong crease.

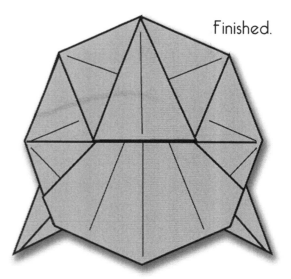

Finished.

design & artwork: Andrew Hudson

NEPHI'S
Ship

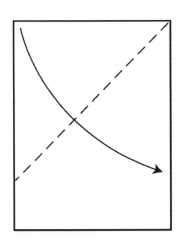

1. Start with a rectangular piece of paper. Fold top left corner down to right side.

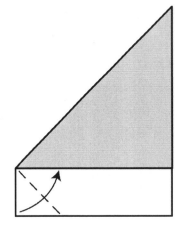

2. Fold bottom corner up.

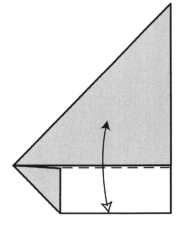

3. Fold bottom flap up & unfold.

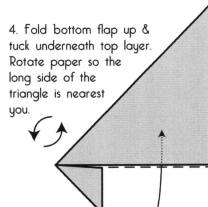

4. Fold bottom flap up & tuck underneath top layer. Rotate paper so the long side of the triangle is nearest you.

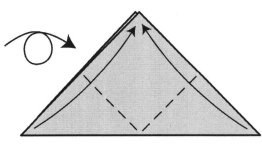

5. Fold bottom corners up to point.

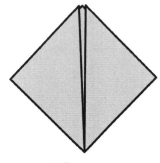

6. Turn over.

NEPHI'S
Ship

DID YOU KNOW:
The four main types of wood used for building where Nephi lived were palm. teak. cedar & mulberry.

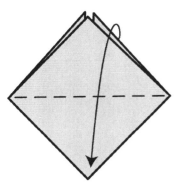

7. Fold top two layers down.

8. Fold right side down then fold up where shown.

9. Tuck fold inside.

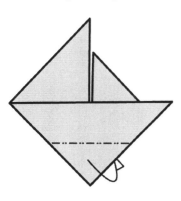

10. Fold bottom point back. Turn over.

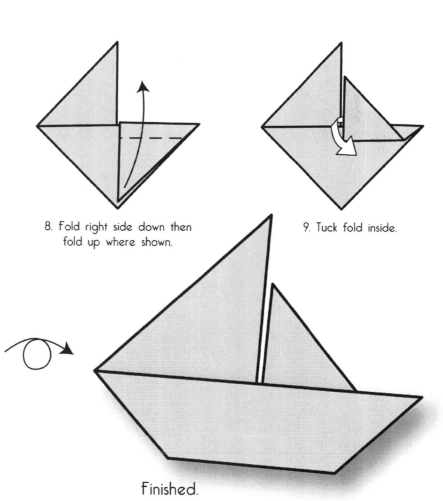

Finished.

artwork: Nick Robinson

KING
Benjamin's Tower

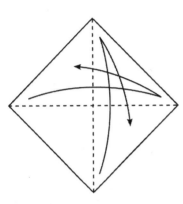

1. Start with a square piece of paper. Fold in half & unfold. Fold in half the other way & unfold.

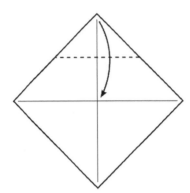

2. Fold top corner to the center & then unfold.

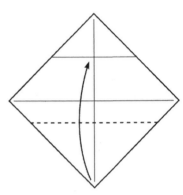

3. Fold bottom corner up to the crease made in step 2.

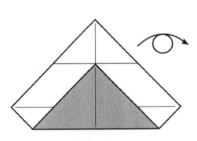

4. Turn over.

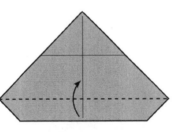

5. Fold flap up.

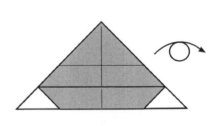

6. Turn over.

16

KING
Benjamin's Tower

skill level: 2

DID YOU KNOW:
King Benjamin's tower was built about 124 years before Jesus Christ was born (124 BC).

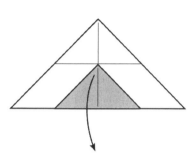

7. Unfold the small triangle.

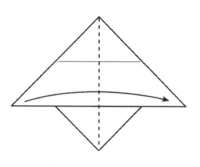

8. Fold in half vertically.

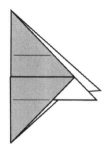

9. First half is finished. Repeat steps 1–8.

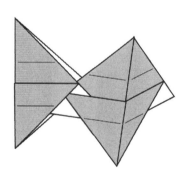

10. Link the halves by sliding ˉarmsˉ of units into each other.

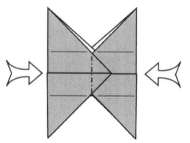

11. Push the two halves together. making sure they do not come apart. Open the model & rotate so your model looks like the picture.

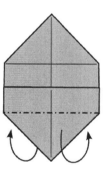

12. Fold the lower points up inside the model to lock them in place. Shape the model so that it is in the shape of a square.

KING
Benjamin's Tower

For the top layer:

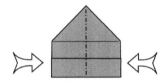

13. Push the sides together again.

14. Fold the points as shown.

15. Push the sides together. leaving the points folded inward.

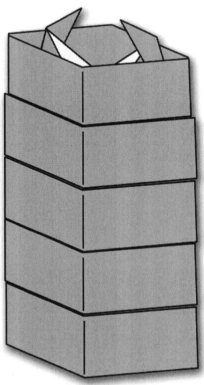

Finished.

16. Top layer finished.

For the bottom layers:

13. Fold the top points inside the model.

14. Push the sides together.

15. Layer finished. Repeat for more layers. Layers may be stacked on top of each other by fitting the top of one layer inside the bottom of another. Stack layers as high as you want your tower to be.

design & artwork: Andrew Hudson

JAREDITE
Barge

QUIZ YOURSELF:
How many days were the
Jaredites upon the water?

See Ether 6:11

1. Start with a square
   piece of paper.
   Fold & unfold.

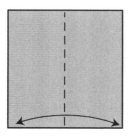

2. Fold left & right sides
   to the middle, then unfold.

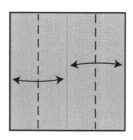

3. Fold top to bottom.

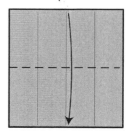

4. Fold & unfold top corners.
   Opening the paper slightly,
   push the corners inside (inside fold).

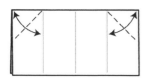

5. Fold top layer
   up to point shown.

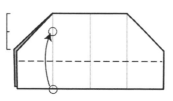

6. Turn over.

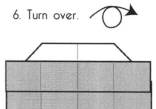

JAREDITE
Barge

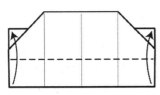

7. Fold top layer up so
it matches other side.

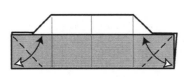

8. Fold & unfold top
layer corners.

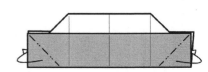

9. Tuck top layer
corners inside.

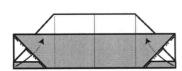

10. Fold bottom layer
corners inside.

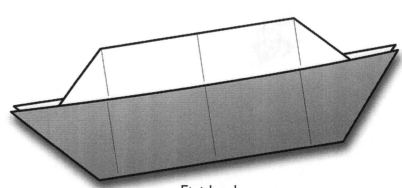

Finished.

artwork: Nick Robinson

NEPHITE
Temple

skill level: 3

DID YOU KNOW?
The Book of Mormon also records that the Lamanites built temples.

Alma 26:29

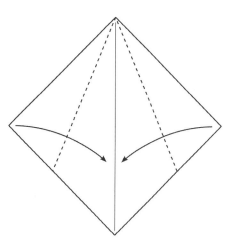

1. Start with a square piece of paper. Fold in half. Fold sides to the middle.

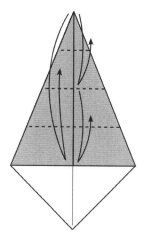

2. Fold & unfold four times.

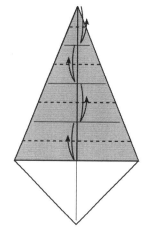

3. Fold & unfold four more times.

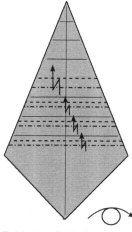

4. Fold & unfold the bottom half so there are eight small sections on the bottom & four large sections on the top. Turn over.

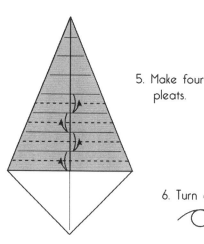

5. Make four pleats.

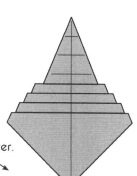

6. Turn over.

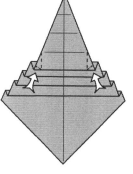

7. Fold sides in & flatten flaps (squash fold) so that the sides are vertical as shown.

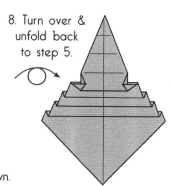

8. Turn over & unfold back to step 5.

QUIZ YOURSELF:

What temple were the people gathered around when the Savior appeared to them?

See 3 Nephi II:I.

NEPHITE
Temple

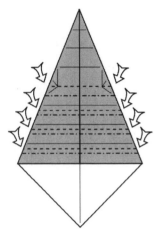

9. Sink the pleats. Notice that the final direction for each crease changes. Remember that dashed lines are valley folds & dotted lines are mountain folds. To the right is a crease pattern for the first one to help you out. You need to reverse the direction of the circled creases on each of the side flaps.

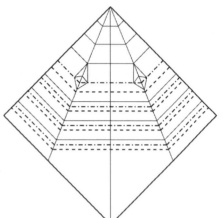

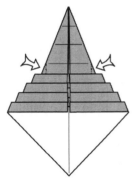

IO. Push the corners inward using the creases from step 7. Again. the image on the right shows which direction the new creases should be.

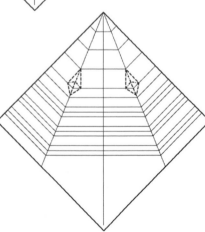

NEPHITE
Temple

QUIZ YOURSELF:
What Old Testament temple did the Nephites pattern their temples after?

See 2 Nephi 5:16.

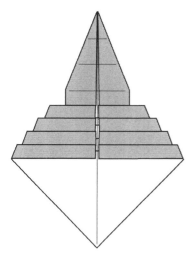

11. Turn over.

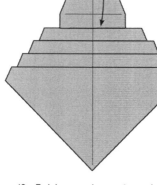

12. Fold top down & tuck in using existing crease.

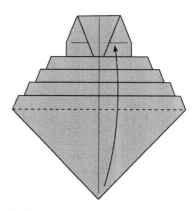

13. Fold bottom flap up as shown.

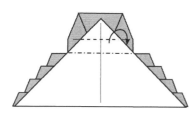

14. Tuck point inside top pleat.

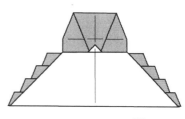

15. Turn over.

QUIZ YOURSELF:

What materials were likely used to build the first Nephite temple?

See 2 Nephi 5:16.

NEPHITE
Temple

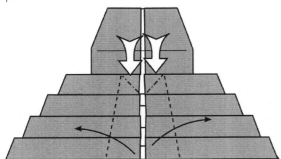

16. Fold flaps open & flatten top of flap (squash fold).

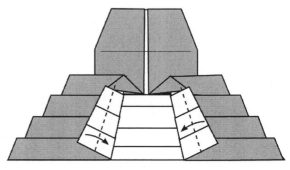

17. Fold over to hide the white part.

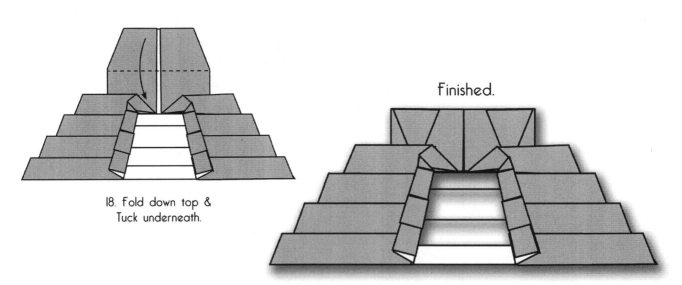

18. Fold down top & Tuck underneath.

Finished.

design & artwork: Andrew Hudson

LEHI'S
Tent

DID YOU KNOW?
Tents in Lehi's time were traditionally made from goat hair woven into fabric.

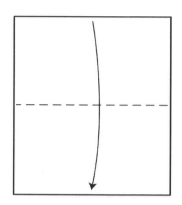

1. Start with a rectangular piece of paper. Fold in half.

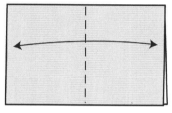

2. Fold in half & unfold.

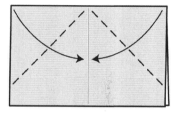

3. Fold top corners down to middle. Crease well.

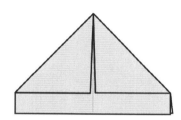

4. Turn paper over.

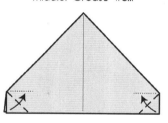

5. Fold bottom corners up.

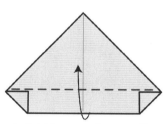

6. Fold bottom flap up. This will help the tent to stand up.

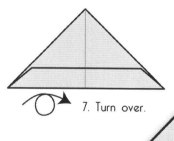

7. Turn over.

8. Fold door flaps out.

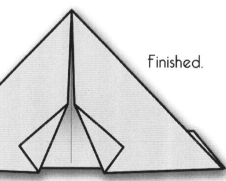

Finished.

artwork: Nick Robinson

CHURCH HISTORY

DESIGNS

CTR
Shield

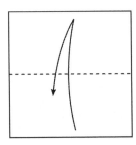

1. Start with a square piece of paper. Fold in half & unfold.

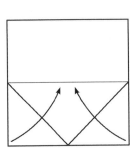

2. Fold bottom corners to middle.

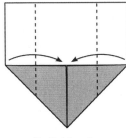

3. Fold sides to middle.

4. Fold and unfold the top two corners.

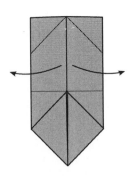

5. Unfold sides from step 3.

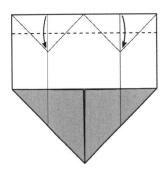

6. Fold top down to the points of triangles.

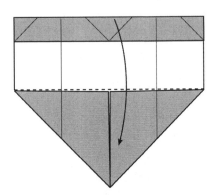

7. Fold top down at center line.

28

CTR
Shield

DID YOU KNOW?
The CTR shield was first incorporated into the Church curriculum in 1970.

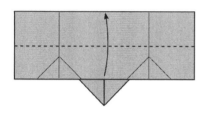

8. Fold top flap up in half.

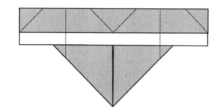

9. Unfold top flap.

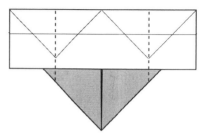

10. Fold sides to the center.

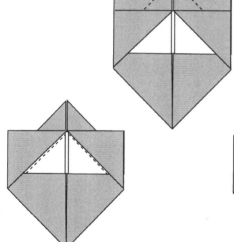

11. Fold top corners forward & inside using existing creases.

12. Tuck flaps up into the pockets.

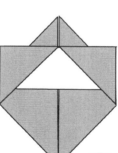

13. Turn over.

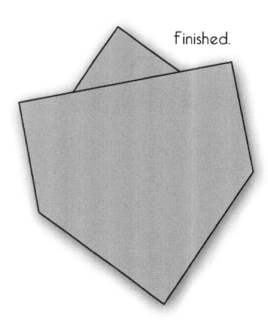

Finished.

design & artwork: Andrew Hudson

WHITE
Shirt

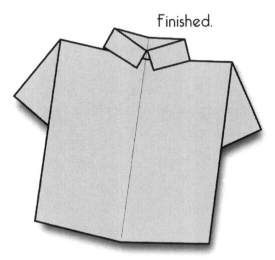

Finished.

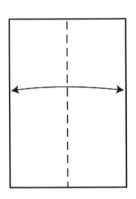

1. Start with a rectangular piece of paper. fold in half & unfold.

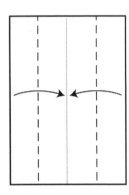

2. fold sides to the middle.

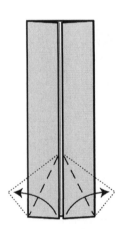

3. Fold top layer corners out.

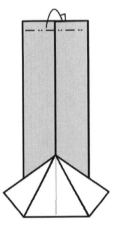

4. Fold top edge behind.

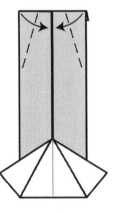

5. Fold top corners forward so their points meet.

6. Fold bottom half up & tuck under collar.

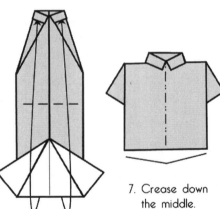

7. Crease down the middle.

artwork: Nick Robinson

30

NECKTIE

DID YOU KNOW:

Over 50 languages are taught in the MTC. & there are 15 MTCs worldwide.

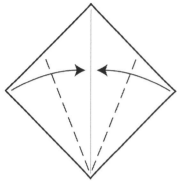

1. Start with a square piece of paper. Fold corners to middle.

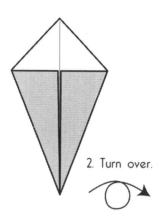

2. Turn over.

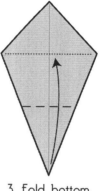

3. Fold bottom point up.

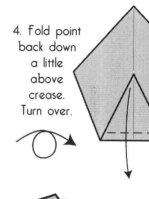

4. Fold point back down a little above crease. Turn over.

5. Fold point up.

6. Fold left sides toward the middle where shown & flatten flap (squash fold). Repeat on right side.

7. Turn over.

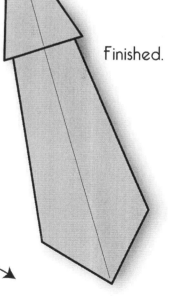

Finished.

artwork: Nick Robinson

31

DID YOU KNOW?

Nearly 3,000 Latter-day Saints traveled by handcart from Iowa & Nebraska to the Salt Lake Valley in a total of 10 handcart companies.

PIONEER
Handcart

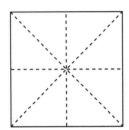

1. Start with a square piece of paper. Fold & unfold: top to bottom, side to side, upper right corner to bottom left corner & upper left corner to bottom right corner.

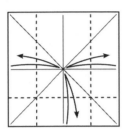

2. Fold & unfold: bottom to middle, left side to middle & right side to middle.

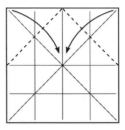

3. Fold top corners to center.

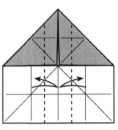

4. Fold & unfold where shown.

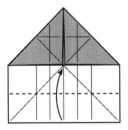

5. Fold bottom to center.

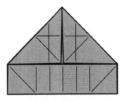

6. Turn over.

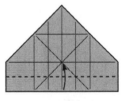

7. Fold bottom to center.

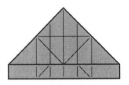

8. Turn over.

PIONEER
Handcart

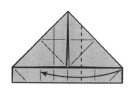

9. Fold right side to crease mark.

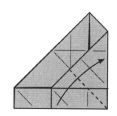

10. Fold top layer to side.

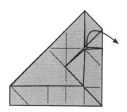

11. Pull out inside layer. Fold point across.

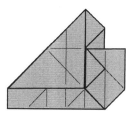

12. Repeat steps 9-11 on the left side.

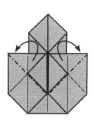

13. Fold top layers behind.

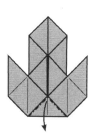

14. Pull out point.

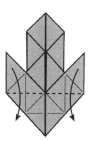

15. Fold down points on each side.

PIONEER
Handcart

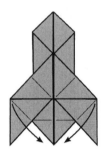

16. Unfold corners.

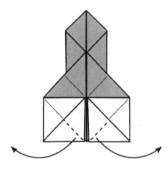

17. Pull corners out.

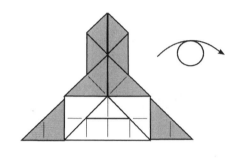

18. Turn over.

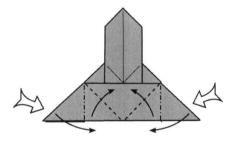

19. Fold corners in (squash fold), making sure when you are done that the point underneath in the middle points down. While folding the top layer of the left square down, flatten the triangular flap to the left.

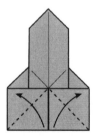

20. Fold middle corners up.

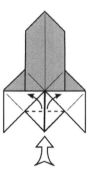

21. Fold bottom point up & flatten (squash fold).

34

PIONEER
Handcart

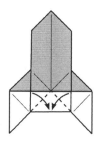

22. Fold small
triangle flaps down.

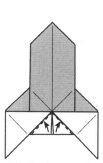

23. Tuck triangle
flaps underneath.

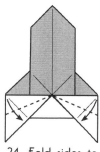

24. Fold sides to
diagnals.

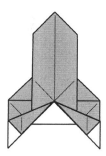

25. Turn over.

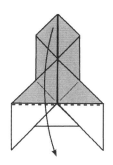

26. Fold down front flap.

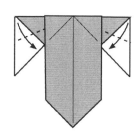

27. Fold top to diagonals.

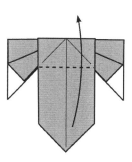

28. Fold front flap up.

35

PIONEER
Handcart

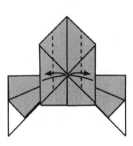

29. Fold & unfold sides.

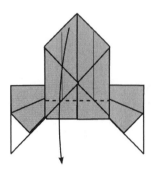

30. Fold down front flap.

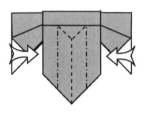

31. Pleat the front flap by pinching the sides together.

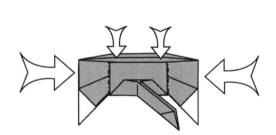

32. Push middle flap down to open model. Crease corners to shape.

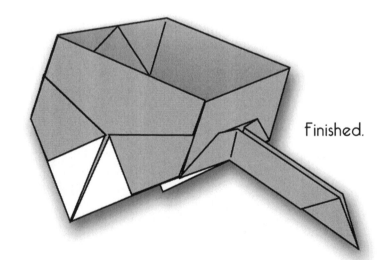

Finished.

design & artwork: Andrew Hudson

COVERED Wagon

DID YOU KNOW?
One pioneer remedy for sores was boiled down beeswax.

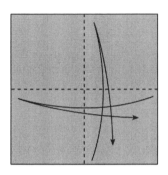

1. Start with a square piece of paper. Fold in half top to bottom & unfold. Fold in half side to side & unfold.

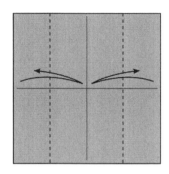

2. Fold left & right sides to middle & unfold.

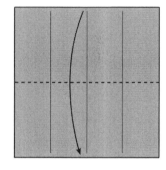

3. Fold in half.

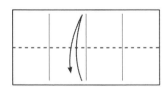

4. Fold top layer up & unfold.

5. Fold top layer up to crease line from step 4.

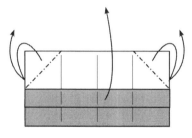

6. Fold top corners back & forth. Then unfold model, leaving step 5 in place.

COVERED
Wagon

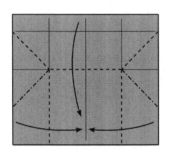

7. Collapse paper on
creases by folding left
& right sides near the
bottom in toward the
middle. This should cause
the top to fold down.

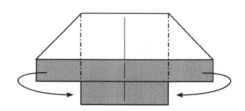

8. Fold sides behind,
then turn paper over.

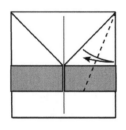

9. Form a crease by
folding & unfolding the
top layer only.

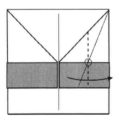

10. Fold top layer over
through circled
intersection.

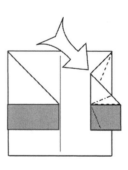

11. Open up top flat
& flatten (squash fold).

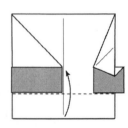

12. Fold bottom
flap up.

COVERED
Wagon

skill level: 2

DID YOU KNOW?
Over 70,000 pioneers traveled over the Oregon-Mormon trail from 1847 to 1869.

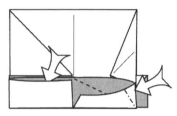

13. Push sides of flap from step 12 toward each other & flatten (double squash fold).

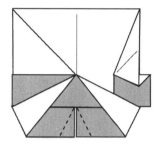

14. Fold bottom flaps up.

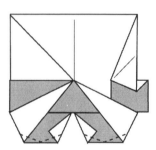

15. Round the wheels then turn the paper over.

Finished.

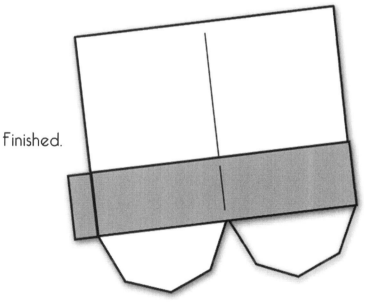

design & artwork: Andrew Hudson

DID YOU KNOW?
Oxen have four parts
to their stomachs.

OX

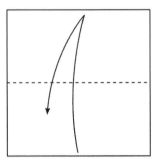

1. Start with a square piece of paper.
Fold in half & unfold.

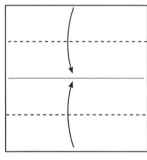

2. Fold top & bottom edges
to the center

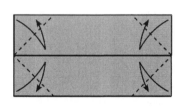

3. Fold & unfold corners to center line.
This will make it easier to fold in step 4.

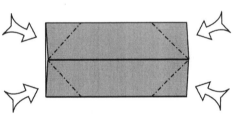

4. Tuck each of the four corners
inside (reverse fold).

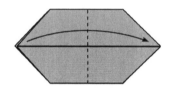

5. Fold in half.

6. Fold right edge of top layer
back, leaving a small gap
before the right edge.

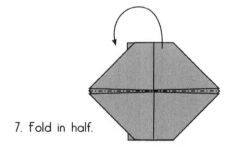

7. Fold in half.

QUIZ YOURSELF:
What is another name
for an ox?

8. Slide the left side up a
little, making a new crease
as you do so.

9. Fold the top & bottom
layers of left side back
as far as they will go.

10. Fold flaps
forward as shown.

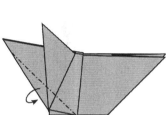

11. Fold top &
bottom layers in.

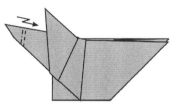

12. Open the model slightly
& pleat the point.

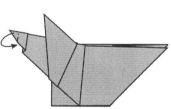

13. Tuck the point inside.

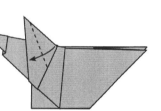

14. Narrow the flap by
folding it forward.

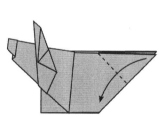

15. Fold the top & bottom
layers of right side down.

OX

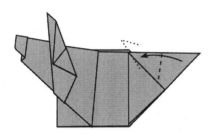

16. Fold the flap on the
right side so it sticks up.

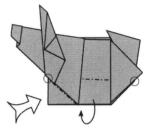

17. Fold the middle up while pushing
in at the large arrow forming
the body as you do so.

18. Unfold step 17.

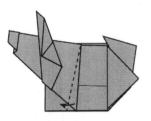

19. Fold the flap forward
at a thin angle.

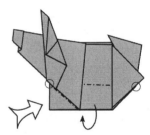

20. Redo fold from step 17.

21. Repeat steps 17-20 on the other side.

OX

QUIZ YOURSELF:

What do the 12 oxen symbolize that are underneath the baptismal fonts in most temples?

ANSWER:

The 12 tribes of Israel. They also signify the strength & power on which God has established His work for the children of mankind.

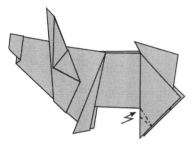

22. Pleat back the rear legs.

23. Crimp the head down. The center will be pushed in between two folds.

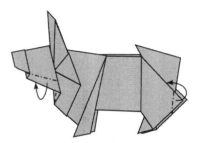

24. Tuck in the bottom edges of the jaw & the rear leg.

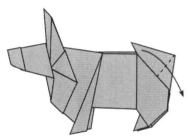

25. Fold the tail out at an angle.

26. Fold the tail down & behind, then curl the horns outward.

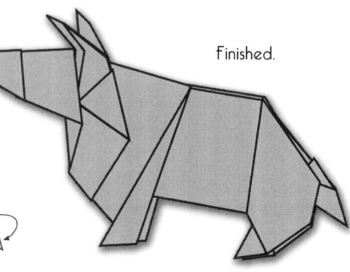

Finished.

design & artwork: Andrew Hudson

STATUE
of Moroni

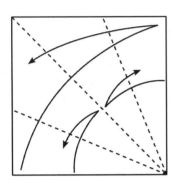

1. Start with a square piece
of paper. Fold in half
diagonally & unfold. Fold
corners to center & unfold.

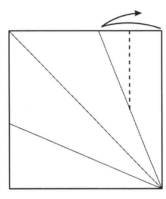

2. Fold right side only down to
the crease line & unfold.

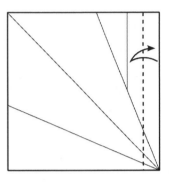

3. Fold right side to crease
line made in step 2
& unfold.

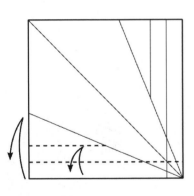

4. Repeat steps 2-3 on
bottom edge.

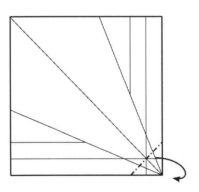

5. Fold bottom right
corner behind.

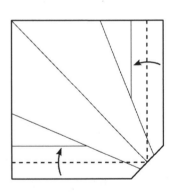

6. Fold right & bottom
edges in.

STATUE
of Moroni

DID YOU KNOW?
The Nauvoo Temple originally had a "statue of Moroni" atop it that was a weather vane cut out of sheet metal.

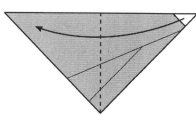

8. Fold in half.

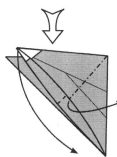
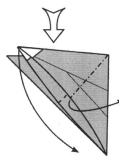

9. Fold the top layer left flap up then flatten the flap (squash fold). It should form a square.

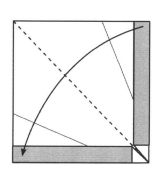

7. Fold in half. Rotate paper so point is near you.

10. Fold flaps to the center & unfold.

11. Fold right side where noted.

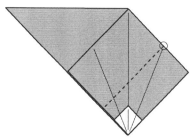

12. Fold top layer flap up then flatten flap (squash fold).

13. Fold & unfold top layer behind the two circled points. This will make it easier to fold in step 14.

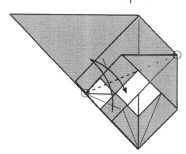

STATUE
of Moroni

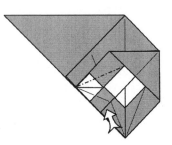

14. Pull the crease from step 13 at
dotted line down & fold the edge
of the paper up (reverse fold).

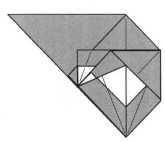

15. Unfold to step 11.

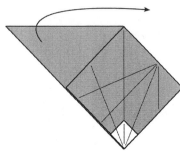

16. Swing the rear flap
to the right side.

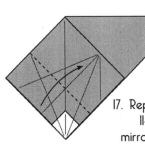

17. Repeat steps
11-14 in
mirror image.

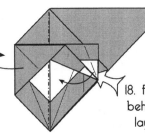

18. Fold the left flap
behind, allowing the
layers to spread.

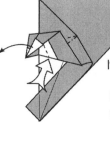

19. Fold the point over
while pushing at the
large arrow & flatten
the flap (squash fold).

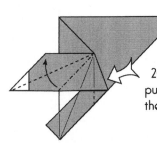

20. Pull up on crease &
push in at arrow to create
the shape shown in step 21.

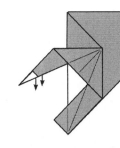

21. Pull out inside layers.
Turn paper over.

STATUE
of Moroni

DID YOU KNOW?

The angel Moroni statues are not solid gold. The final casing is covered with two thin layers of gold leaf.

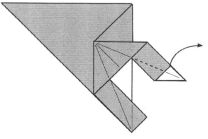

22. Pull out the corner of the paper as far as it will go.

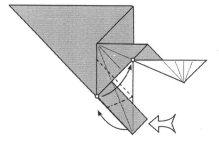

23. Fold the head flap so that the left corner hits the center & flatten it (squash fold). Repeat behind.

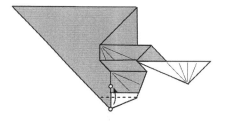

24. Fold bottom edge up. Repeat behind.

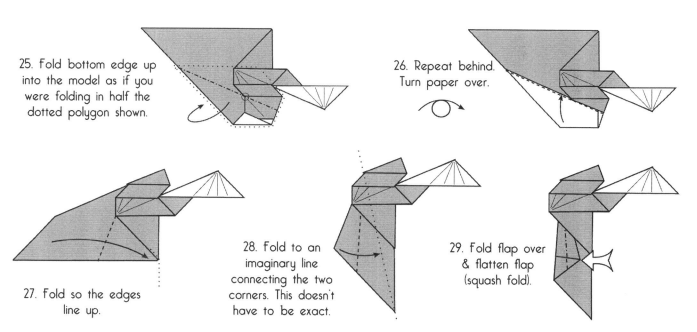

25. Fold bottom edge up into the model as if you were folding in half the dotted polygon shown.

26. Repeat behind. Turn paper over.

27. Fold so the edges line up.

28. Fold to an imaginary line connecting the two corners. This doesn't have to be exact.

29. Fold flap over & flatten flap (squash fold).

47

STATUE
of Moroni

QUIZ YOURSELF:

Which direction do the angel
Moroni statues on temples usuallly face?

ANSWER:

East.

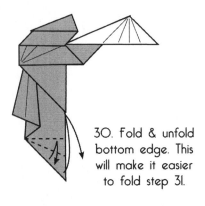

30. Fold & unfold
bottom edge. This
will make it easier
to fold step 31.

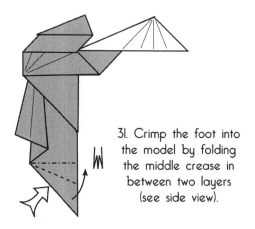

31. Crimp the foot into
the model by folding
the middle crease in
between two layers
(see side view).

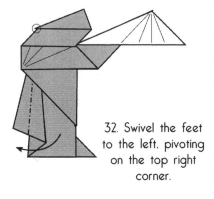

32. Swivel the feet
to the left. pivoting
on the top right
corner.

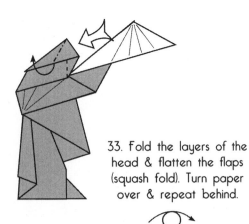

33. Fold the layers of the
head & flatten the flaps
(squash fold). Turn paper
over & repeat behind.

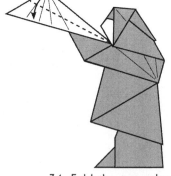

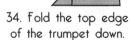

34. Fold the top edge
of the trumpet down.

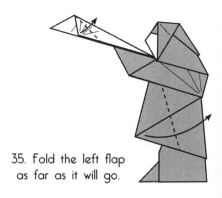

35. Fold the left flap
as far as it will go.

STATUE
of Moroni

DID YOU KNOW:
A heavy weight attached to the statue's feet is suspended inside the temple spire where Moroni is standing so the statue can move slightly in the wind without breaking.

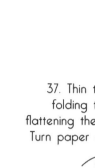

36. Shape the tip of the trumpet.

37. Thin the arms by folding the flaps & flattening them (squash fold). Turn paper over & repeat.

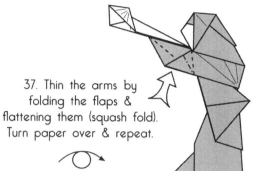

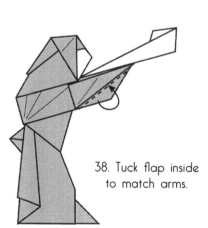

38. Tuck flap inside to match arms.

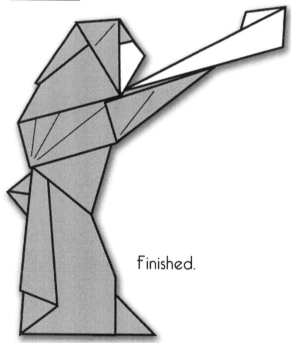

Finished.

design & artwork: Andrew Hudson

LATTER-DAY TEMPLE

DESIGNS

TEMPLE
Salt Lake

DID YOU KNOW?
Announcement: 28 July 1847
Site Dedication: 14 February 1853
        by Heber C. Kimball
Dedication: 6-24 April 1893
        by Wilford Woodruff

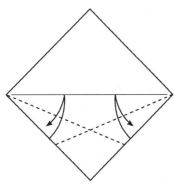

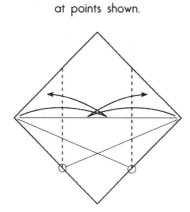

2. Fold & unfold
at points shown.

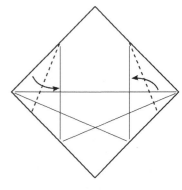

1. Start with a square piece of paper.
Fold in half & unfold. Fold bottom point
to center both ways as shown & unfold.

3. Fold sides in.

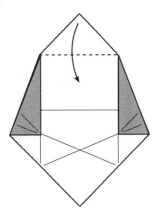

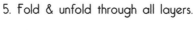

5. Fold & unfold through all layers.

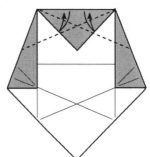

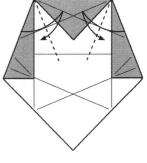

4. Fold top down.

6. Fold & unfold sides.

TEMPLE
Salt Lake

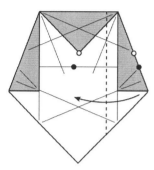

7. Fold right side over lining up the two reference points.

8. Circled intersections should line up. Fold left side over.

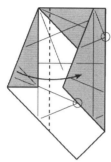

9. Turn paper over.

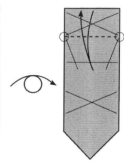

10. Fold & unfold through all layers then turn paper over & unfold to step 7.

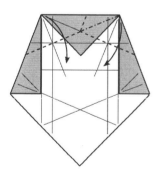

11. Fold top corners in. This will create a flap in the center. Fold center flap to the right.

12. Fold center flap up then flatten the flap in the center (squash fold).

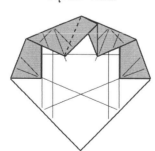

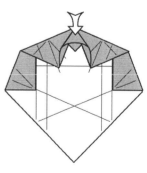

13. Squash fold in progress

DID YOU KNOW:
The Salt Lake Temple was the only temple dedicated by President Wilford Woodruff.

TEMPLE
Salt Lake

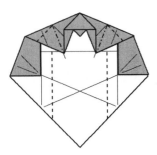

14. Fold sides in, tucking the sides underneath the top flaps.

15. Fold top layers behind on the crease so the two towers stand up.

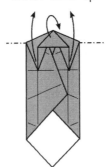

16. Fold in half & unfold.

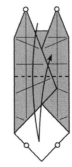

17. Fold & unfold on the bottom half of the model to establish creases.

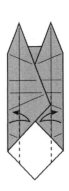

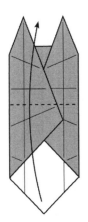

18. Fold bottom up. Turn paper over.

19. Fold sides inside the model using existing creases.

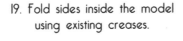

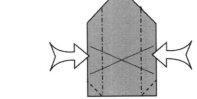

20. Turn paper over.

21. Fold two points down.

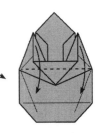

54

TEMPLE
Salt Lake

DID YOU KNOW?
The Salt Lake Temple is the first temple to feature a standing angel Moroni statue, which was created by Paris-trained sculptor Cyrus E. Dallin.

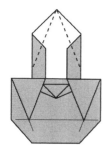

22. Thin the middle point by folding the sides in.

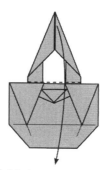

23. Fold the top point down.

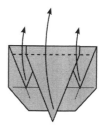

24. Fold all three points up.

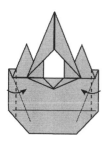

25. Fold in the sides to lock step 24 shut.

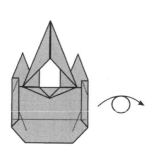

26. Turn paper over.

Finished.

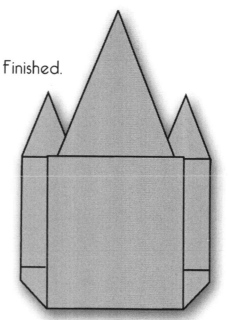

design & artwork: Andrew Hudson

TEMPLE
Mesa Arizona

DID YOU KNOW:
Announcement: 3 October 1919
Site Dedication: 28 November 1921
    by Heber J. Grant
Dedication: 23-26 October 1927
    by Heber J. Grant

1. Start with a square piece of paper. Fold & unfold top to bottom & side to side.

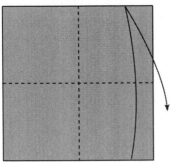

2. Fold top & bottom to middle & unfold.

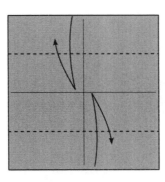

3. Fold & unfold left & right sides to center four times, making a total of 16 sections.

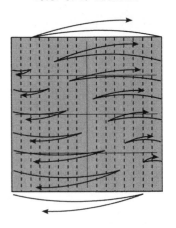

4. Pleat both sides at the third crease from the left & the right side.

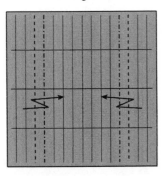

5. Fold top & bottom back on the creases made in step 2.

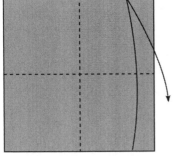

6. Fold the top & bottom edges inward.

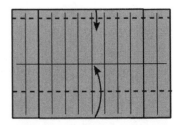

TEMPLE
Mesa Arizona

skill level: 2
DID YOU KNOW?

The Easter season brings thousands of guests to the Mesa Arizona Temple grounds every year to watch *Jesus the Christ*, the largest annual outdoor Easter pageant in the world.

7. Turn paper over.

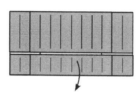

8. Unfold the bottom.

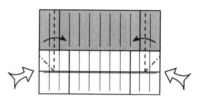

9. Fold left side in & flatten flap (squash fold). Repeat on right side.

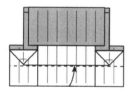

10. Fold lower layer back up & under flap.

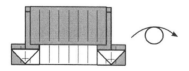

11. Turn paper over.

Finished.

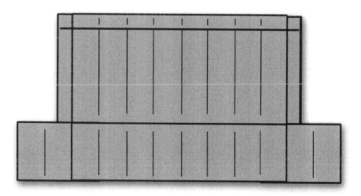

design & artwork: Andrew Hudson

DID YOU KNOW:
Announcement: 4 October 2008
Site Dedication: 8 May 2010
        by Ronald A. Rasband
Dedication: 6 May 2012
        by Thomas S. Monson

TEMPLE
Kansas City Missouri

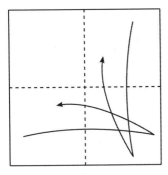

1. Start with a square piece of paper. Fold & unfold top to bottom & side to side.

2. Fold sides to the middle & unfold.

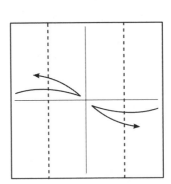

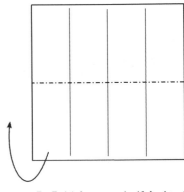

3. Fold bottom half behind.

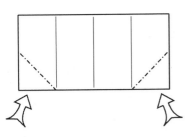

4. Fold bottom corners back & forth. then. opening the paper slightly. push the corners inside (inside fold).

5. Fold top flaps down on front & back.

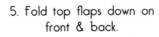

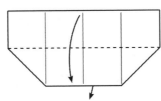

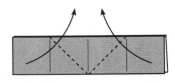

6. Fold sides up to center.

58

TEMPLE
Kansas City Missouri

skill level: 2

DID YOU KNOW:
The Kansas City Missouri Temple will be the second temple built in Missouri. Following the St. Louis Missouri Temple (1997).

7. Fold top layer down.

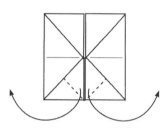

8. Pull out corners & flatten.

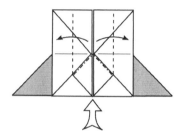

9. Fold center flaps outward while allowing bottom point to fold up. Flatten point (squash fold).

10. Fold corners in.

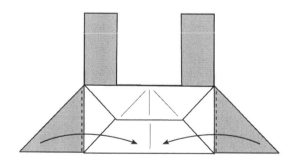

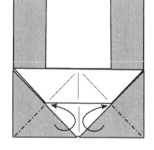

11. Tuck flaps from step 10 in pockets.

12. Fold & unfold towers down as shown.

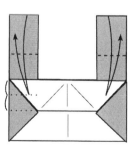

TEMPLE
Kansas City Missouri

DID YOU KNOW?

Beautiful white oak harvested from Adam-ondi-Ahman was used throughout the interior of the Kansas City Missouri Temple.

13. Pleat towers in half.

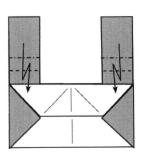

14. Fold outside edges of towers in.

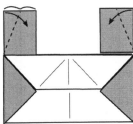

15. Fold inside edges of towers in.

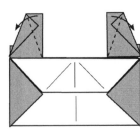

16. Tuck flaps behind.

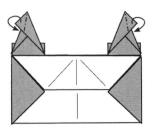

17. Turn paper over.

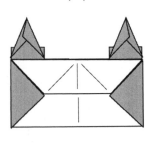

Finished.

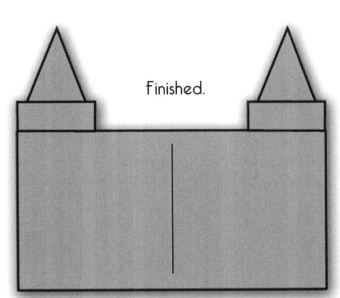

design & artwork: Andrew Hudson

TEMPLE
Toronto Ontario

skill level: 2

DID YOU KNOW:
Announcement: 7 April 1984
Site Dedication: 10 October 1987
by Thomas S. Monson
Dedication: 25-27 August 1990
by Gordon B. Hinckley

1. Start with a square piece of paper. Fold ih half on diagonal & unfold. Fold corners to center.

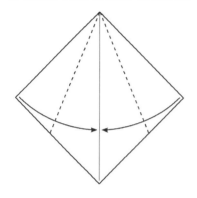

2. Fold in half & unfold.

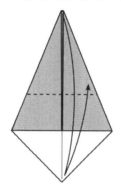

3. Fold bottom flap up to crease from step 2 & unfold.

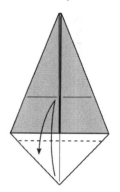

4. Pleat down to the edge.

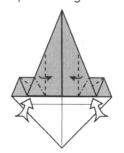

5. Fold left edge in & flatten flap (squash fold). Repeat on right side.

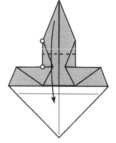

6. Fold top down. being sure to match at points shown.

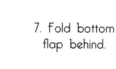

7. Fold bottom flap behind.

DID YOU KNOW?
Dedication proceedings were translated into French—one of Canada's official languages—and into Spanish, Portuguese, Mandarin, Cantonese & Korean.

TEMPLE
Toronto Ontario

8. Fold flap back up, being sure to match at paints shown.

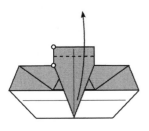

9. Fold left side in & flatten flap (squash fold). Repeat on right side.

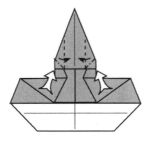

10. Fold edges in to thin the steeple.

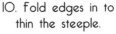
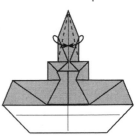

Finished.

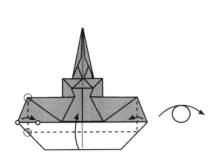

11. Fold sides & bottom in to form a square base. Turn paper over.

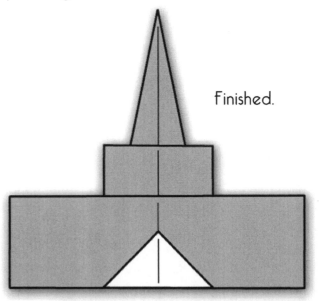

design & artwork: Andrew Hudson

TEMPLE
Nauvoo Illinois

skill level: 2

DID YOU KNOW?

Announcement: 4 April 1999
Site Dedication: 24 October 1999
by Gordon B. Hinckley
Dedication: 27-30 June 2002
by Gordon B. Hinckley

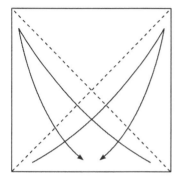

1. Start with a square piece of paper. Fold in half diagonally both ways & unfold.

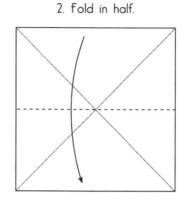

2. Fold in half.

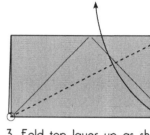

3. Fold top layer up as shown.

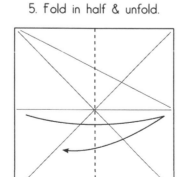

4. Unfold paper.

5. Fold in half & unfold.

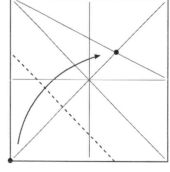

6. Fold bottom left corner to where the creases meet.

TEMPLE
Nauvoo Illinois

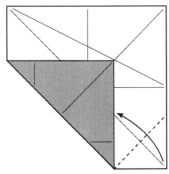

7. Fold bottom right corner
up to meet edge.

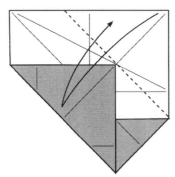

8. Fold & unfold
top right corner.

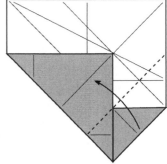

9. Fold bottom right
edge to center.

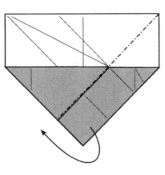

10. Fold bottom right
edge behind.

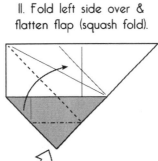
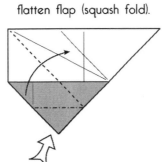

11. Fold left side over &
flatten flap (squash fold).

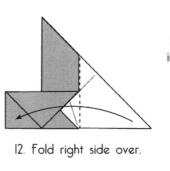

12. Fold right side over.

13. Tuck flap
inside pocket.

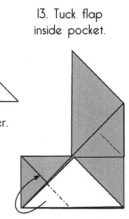

TEMPLE
Nauvoo Illinois

DID YOU KNOW:
The Nauvoo Illinois Temple is a reconstruction of the original Nauvoo Temple built in the 1840s & destroyed by fire in 1848.

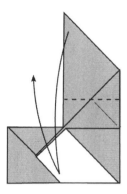

14. Fold top in half & unfold.

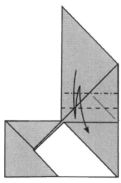
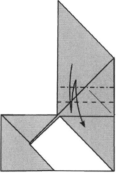
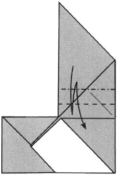
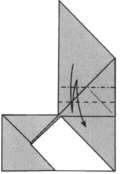

15. Pleat flap down.

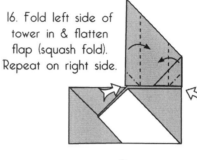

16. Fold left side of tower in & flatten flap (squash fold). Repeat on right side.

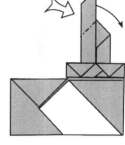

17. Fold tallest tower back & to the right.

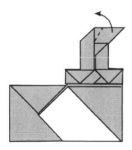

18. Fold spire up.

19. Turn paper over.

Finished.

design & artwork: Andrew Hudson

65

TEMPLE
Accra Ghana

DID YOU KNOW:
Announcement: 16 February 1998
Site Dedication: 16 November 2001
    by Russell M Nelson
Dedication: 11 January 2004
    by Gordon B. Hinckley

1. Start with a square piece of paper.
Fold side corners to center.

2. Fold top down.

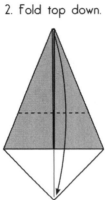

3. Fold top layer
up. then unfold.

4. Fold up at dashed line.
lining up crease from step
three with edge of paper.

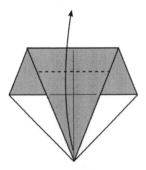

5. Fold bottom up.

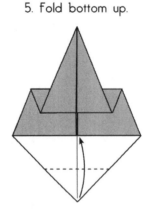

6. Fold bottom up
& underneath.

66

TEMPLE
Accra Ghana

skill level: 2

DID YOU KNOW?
Missionaries first entered Ghana in 1978.

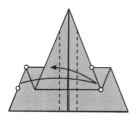

7. Fold & unfold both sides matching points shown.

8. Fold sides in.

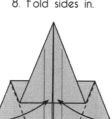

9. Fold left flap up. then open & flatten flap (squash fold) creating a straight side. Repeat on right side.

10. Bring middle layer in front of flaps from step 9.

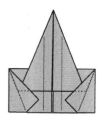

11. Fold top layer along the edge of the lower layer from step 9.

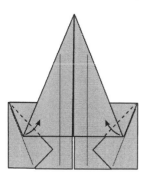

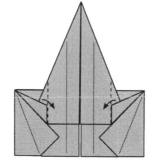

12. Pull bottom layer out & flatten. This will thin the tower slightly.

13. Pleat sides in using the existing line as the inside crease.

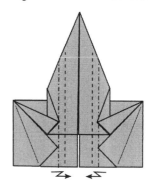

DID YOU KNOW?

The Accra Ghana Temple was the first temple built in West Africa & the second built in Africa, following the Johannesburg South Africa Temple.

TEMPLE
Accra Ghana

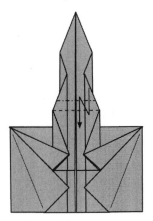

14. Pleat tower down.

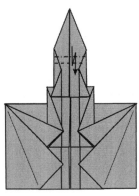

15. Pleat tower down again.

16. Fold left side in & flatten flap (squash fold). Repeat on right side.

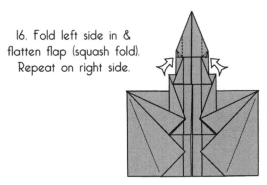

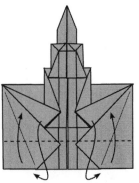

17. Fold bottom edge up & tuck under flap to lock.

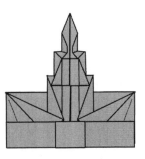

18. Turn paper over.

Finished.

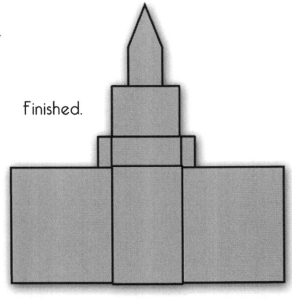

design & artwork: Andrew Hudson

68

TEMPLE
Copenhagen Denmark

skill level: 3

DID YOU KNOW?
Announcement: 17 March 1999
Site Dedication: 24 April 1999
by Spencer J. Condie
Dedication: 23 May 2004
by Gordon B. Hinckley

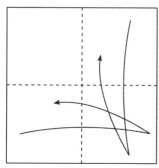

1. Start with a square piece of paper. Fold & unfold top to bottom & side to side.

2. Fold sides to center & unfold.

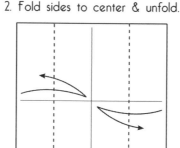
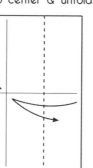

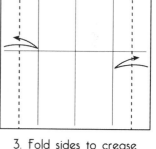

3. Fold sides to crease from step 2 & unfold.

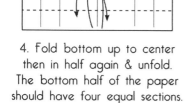

4. Fold bottom up to center then in half again & unfold. The bottom half of the paper should have four equal sections.

5. Fold bottom corners in.

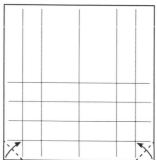

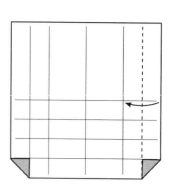

6. Fold right edge in.

TEMPLE
Copenhagen Denmark

7. Fold top right corner down.

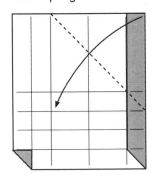

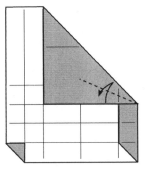

8. Crease on right side where shown.

9. Crease on top where shown.

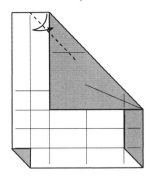

10. Make second crease on top where shown.

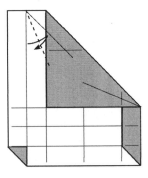

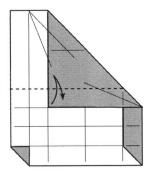

11. Fold top down & unfold. Be sure to crease through all layers.

12. Fold a line connecting the two points & unfold.

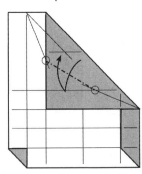

TEMPLE
Copenhagen Denmark

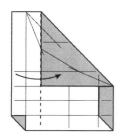

13. Fold left side over.

14. Pleat top down.

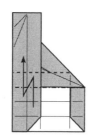

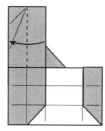

15. Fold tower to the left while flattening fold (squash fold) behind pleat fron step 14.

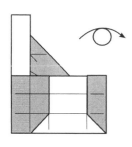

16. Turn paper over.

17. Pull down on crease from step 12. Model will not lie flat.

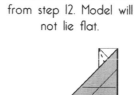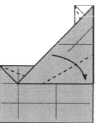

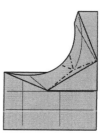

18. Flatten into place. starting from the outside & working your way inward using the creases you made in steps 8-10. Note: This is a difficult step that may take some practice but. when done correctly. will fold properly into palce.

TEMPLE
Copenhagen Denmark

DID YOU KNOW?

The Copenhagen Denmark Temple was built from an existing building. The temple was built out of the Priorvej chapel. which was originally built in 1931.

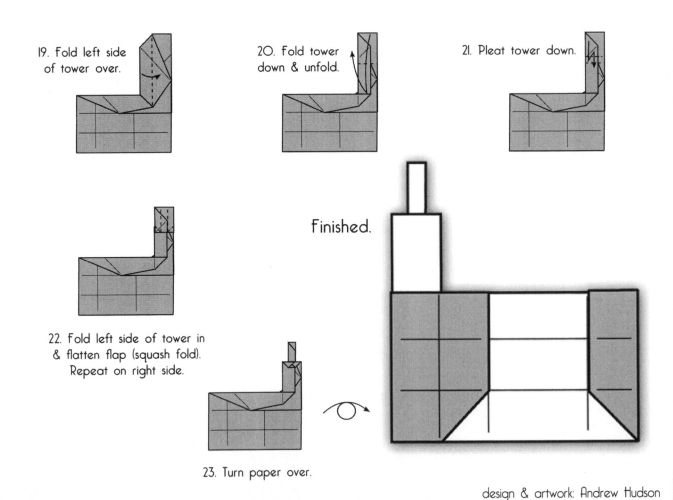

19. Fold left side of tower over.

20. Fold tower down & unfold.

21. Pleat tower down.

22. Fold left side of tower in & flatten flap (squash fold). Repeat on right side.

23. Turn paper over.

Finished.

design & artwork: Andrew Hudson

72

TEMPLE
London England

skill level: 3

DID YOU KNOW?
Announcement: 17 February 1955
Site Dedication: 10 August 1953
by David O. McKay
Dedication: 7-9 September 1958
by David O. McKay

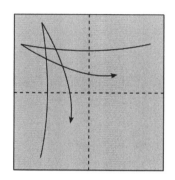

1. Start with a square piece of paper. Fold in half top to bottom & side to side. then unfold.

2. Fold top & bottom to center & unfold. Turn paper over.

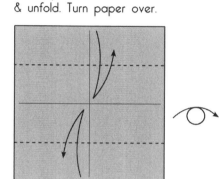

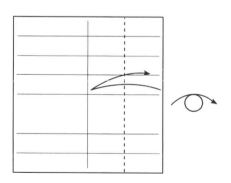

3. Fold bottom up & unfold. Fold top down twice as shown & unfold.

4. Fold right side to middle & unfold. Turn paper over.

5. Fold left side twice as shown & unfold.

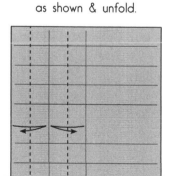

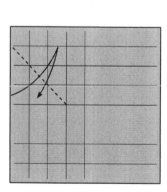

6. Fold the left edge to the first crease & unfold.

TEMPLE
London England

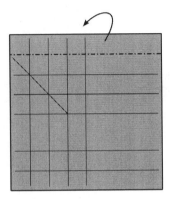

7. Fold top edge back.

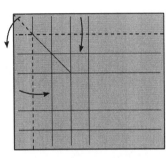

8. "Rabbitear" by folding the top & the left side inward so that the tower extends out to the left.

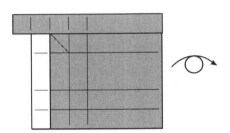

9. Turn paper over.

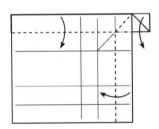

10. "Rabbitear" again by folding the top & the right side inward so that the tower extends out to the right.

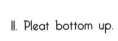

11. Pleat bottom up.

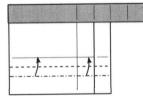

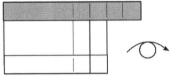

12. Turn paper over.

13. Fold right edge in flatten flap on bottom (squash fold).

TEMPLE
London England

skill level: 3

DID YOU KNOW?

The site where the London England Temple stands, known as Newchapel Farm, was listed in the *Domesday Book* of William the Conquerer.

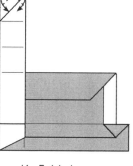

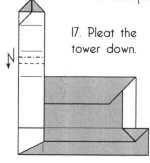

17. Pleat the tower down.

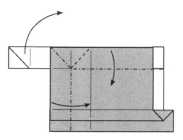

14. "Rabbitear" again folding the top & the left sides inward this time so the tower extends up.

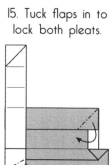

15. Tuck flaps in to lock both pleats.

16. Fold the top corners down.

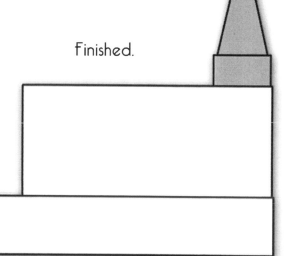

Finished.

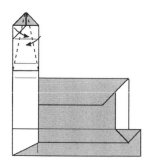

18. Fold edges in to thin the steeple.

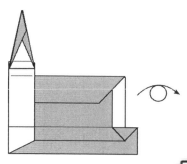

19. Turn paper over.

design & artwork: Andrew Hudson

TEMPLE
Hong Kong China

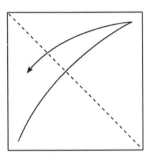

1. Start with a square piece of paper. Fold in half & unfold.

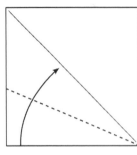

2. Fold bottom edge to diagonal crease.

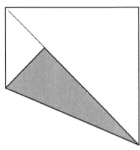

3. Turn paper over.

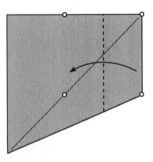

4. Fold right edge over so the points line up as shown.

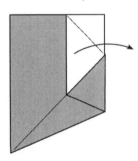

5. Unfold step 4.

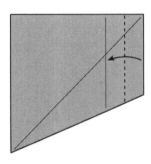

6. Fold right side over to the crease from step 4.

TEMPLE
Hong Kong China

skill level: 2

DID YOU KNOW?
The Hong Kong China Temple was the first high-rise temple built by the Church.

7. Fold bottom up.

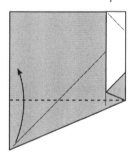

8. Fold top down through points shown.

9. Fold top layer up & unfold.

10. Fold top layer up where shown.

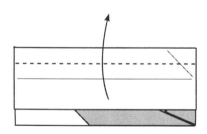

11. Fold in half & unfold.

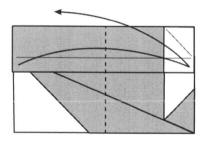

12. Pleat by bringing right side over & matching points shown.

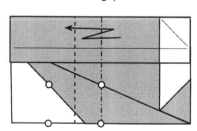

TEMPLE
Hong Kong China

13. Fold top corner back to lock the pleat.

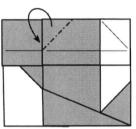

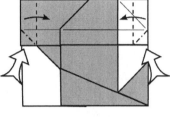

14. Fold left side in & flatten flap (squash fold). Repeat on right side.

15. Turn paper over.

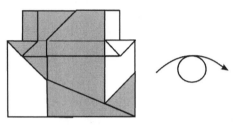

16. Fold point behind.

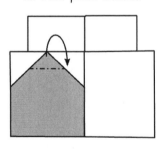

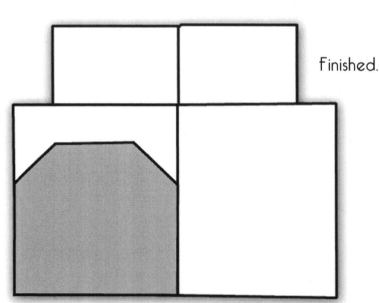

Finished.

design & artwork: Andrew Hudson

TEMPLE
Papeete Tahiti

skill level: 3

DID YOU KNOW?
Announcement: 2 April. 1980
Site Dedication: 13 February 1981
by Spencer W. Kimball
Dedication: 27-29 October 1983
by Gordon B. Hinckley

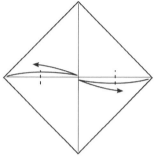

1. Start with a square piece of paper.
Fold in half diagonally & unfold.
Fold in half diagonally the
other direction & unfold.

2. Fold & unfold sides to
establish creases where shown.

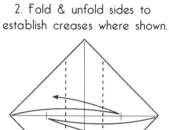

3. Fold sides down to
creases from step 2.

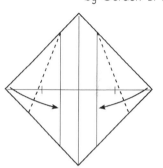

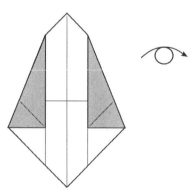

4. Turn paper over.

5. Make a small
pleat up.

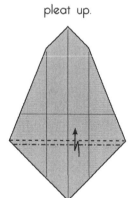

6. Pleat the lines from
step 2 to center.

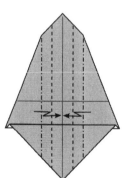

DID YOU KNOW?

Tahiti's second stake was organized just one year before the Papeete Tahiti Temple was dedicated.

TEMPLE
Papeete Tahiti

7. Fold & unfold along the edge of the layers behind.

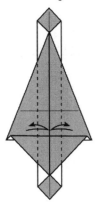

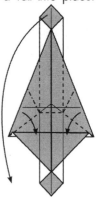

8. Fold outer edges to the horizontal line.

9. Using creases from steps 7 & 8, fold down slowly as shown. The other creases should fold inward & fall into place.

10. Fold bottom flap up

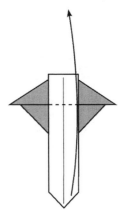

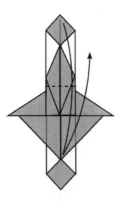

11. Fold & unfold sides to form creases where shown.

12. Fold & unfold to form creases where shown.

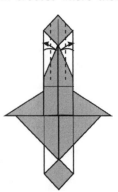

TEMPLE
Papeete Tahiti

DID YOU KNOW?

In 2005, this temple was renovated, adding over 2,000 square feet. It was then rededicated.

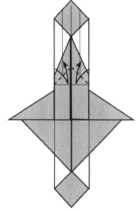

13. Fold and unfold to form two creases as shown.

14. Pleat tower down through the intersections from steps 12 & 13.

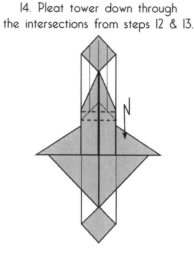

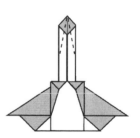

15. Fold left side in & flatten flap (squash fold). Repeat on right side.

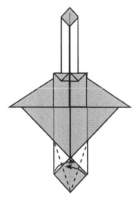

16. Fold bottom sides in. They will overlap.

17. Fold bottom up & tuck inside top flap.

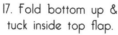

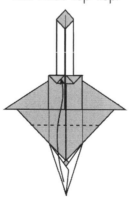

18. Fold sides of tower in.

TEMPLE
Papeete Tahiti

Before the Papeete temple was built, how many miles did the Saints have to travel to attend the temple?

ANSWER:
2,500 miles to Hamilton, New Zealand.

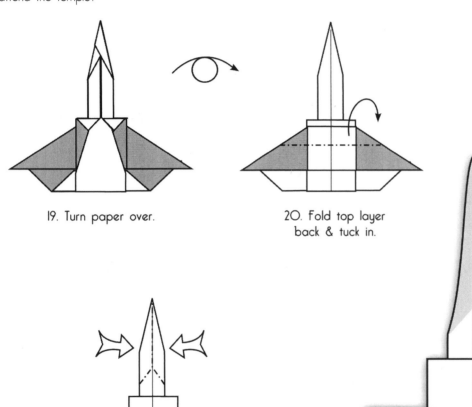

19. Turn paper over.

20. Fold top layer back & tuck in.

21. Pinch to shape the tower.

Finished.

design & artwork: Andrew Hudson

82

INDEX
BY SKILL LEVEL

ABOUT THE AUTHOR

Todd Huisken is a licensed marriage & family therapist & a counseling manager in Fountain Valley, California. He attended Brigham Young University & the University of San Diego & has a master's degree in marriage & family therapy. Todd has served as the assistant director of Disaster Mental Health Services for the Orange County chapter of the American Red Cross. He has worked with victims from the San Diego Fires & Hurricanes Ivan & Katrina, & he spent two weeks in Haiti after the devastating earthquake in 2010.

Todd was an early morning seminary teacher for six years. He is the author of *The Dating Directory* & the founder of *Process and Content*, a graduate program newsletter at the University of San Diego. Most important, Todd has been married to his beautiful wife for twenty-three years, & they have three daughters & a son. The Huiskens try to make Disneyland their second home.